Reflections

First published in 2025 by Alyson Torns Publishing.
Alyson Torns Publishing is an imprint of Libri Publishing.
Copyright © Alyson Torns

The right of Alyson Torns to be identified as the author of this work has been asserted in accordance with the Copyright, Designs and Patents Act, 1988. Views expressed are those of the author alone.
ISBN 978-1-912969-77-7

All rights reserved. No part of this publication may be reproduced, stored in any retrieval system or transmitted in any form or by any means, electronic, mechanical, photocopying, recording or otherwise, without the prior written permission of the copyright holder for which application should be addressed in the first instance to the publishers. No liability shall be attached to the author, the copyright holder or the publishers for loss or damage of any nature suffered as a result of reliance on the reproduction of any of the contents of this publication or any errors or omissions in its contents.

A CIP catalogue record for this book is available from The British Library

Design by Carnegie Book Production

Libri Publishing
Brunel House
Volunteer Way
Faringdon
Oxfordshire
SN7 7YR

Tel: +44 (0)845 873 3837

www.libripublishing.co.uk

Reflections
a window into a life

written and illustrated by

Alyson Torns

DEDICATION

For all the strangers I have met

Thank you to my Dad and Lynnette for supporting me.

PUBLICATIONS

Alyson Torns most recent publication was called 'There's No Wi-If: 151 Poems In A Week Of Regeneration' published by Mardibooks Kindle Edition 2019.

'Unresolved Journey' was published by Mardibooks Kindle Edition 2012

'From The Lost Property Office: a quartet for Pessoa' published by Hearing Eye, 2006.

Alyson has had poems and paintings published in The Otolith, Past Simple, Great Works, Veer Off, Poetry Salsburg Review, Poetry London, The Interpreter's House, Fire, The Wolf, Neon Highway, Hanging Johnny and Tears in the Fence.

Her paintings have been shown in the Pallant Gallery, 2009; The Kings Place Guardian Gallery 2011 and included in the Museum of Everything #2book, published in 2010 and in the Outside in gallery.

I wrote these poems as a way of processing my thoughts and feelings over the last 5 years. These poems were written during 2019-2023 as meditative, moments captured through the rear-view mirror.

Snap shots, fragments and pauses as my personal journey evolves and unfolds.

My creativity allows me to articulate thoughts and feelings. The poems and artwork included in this collection enable me to continue to grow as a person. I feel my poems are a gift. They are authentic journeys in their own episodes and experiences. They enable my ongoing journey of recovery.

Poetry creates a language which helps us verbalise emotions and metamorphose.

I've worked for the last 6 years for a mental health charity, supporting adults with mental health problems. Some of these poems were written in creative writing sessions, which I run for people on a 1:1 basis or within a group setting. It astounds me how willing the clients are to write and share their words with me and the group.

The writing enables people to find a voice and verbalise emotions that they couldn't otherwise do. There is a collective energy when a group of people come together or one to one and write in silence. It's magical to watch people blossom and grow in confidence.

I hope these poems inspire you in some way to find your own creative voice.

These mini awarenesses help my on-going development as a writer, a poet, a woman, and fundamentally as a human being.

The artworks in the book were captured on a daily basis through a period of time.

Alyson Torns

my whole life
is behind
cupboards
years of journals
piled on top
of one another
never read back
but there as
an account of
a life lived
in isolation
fear of opening
the doors unsure
of what i will find
words etched
on lines
with pictures
showing a life
journey
this has been
a salvation
a documentary
of a life lived
behind closed
doors

surrounded
but invisible to all
small child
hiding inside
scared
to speak up
to unsettle
the joy
sacrificed
herself
for what

we carry our
wounds like we
carry our words

this void
can't be ignored
this aching
grief
always
beneath the
surface
comes with
no warning
powerless

that energy
that can't be seen
or touched
by hand
yet presents
itself to me
daily through
the strangers i meet
when i feel
most defeated

reparenting myself
no role model
hand it over

anxiety rises
flooded
hand on heart

knowing you're there
brings joy
to a broken heart

how do i detach
myself from you
by letting go
of control

giving a gift
to someone
priceless

feeling grounded
momentarily
breathe

feeling angry
overwhelmed
turbulence

feeling rested
capture
this moment

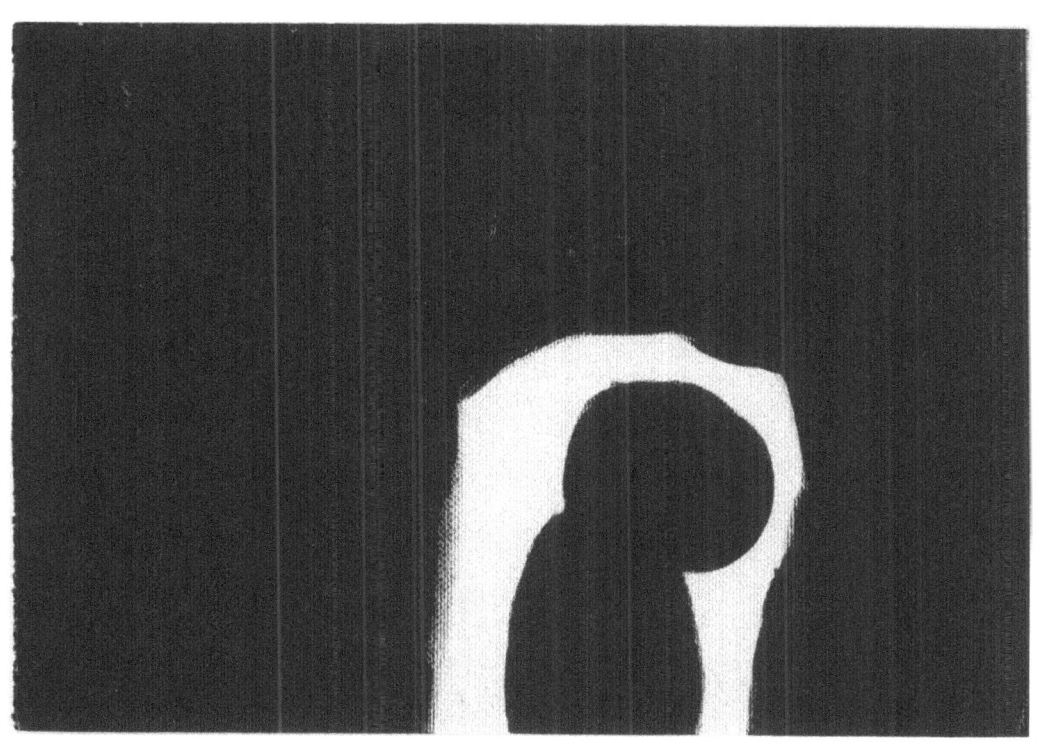

today words
fail to come
solitary
lockdown
speechless

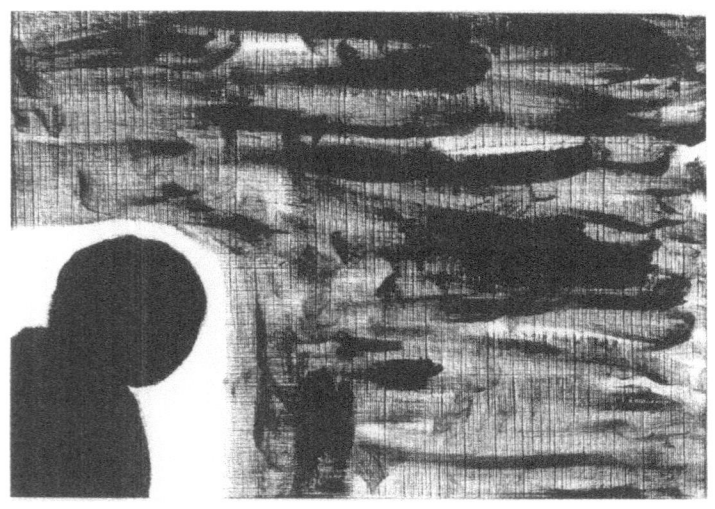

foundations
destabilised
disquiet
sits
in stomach
surrounded
families
at war
with each other
collateral
damage
children
left alone
on street
wailing

how long
will this last
till we feel
human touch
again
need
to be held

raw
in the pit
of my
stomach
emotions
stirred
need
help

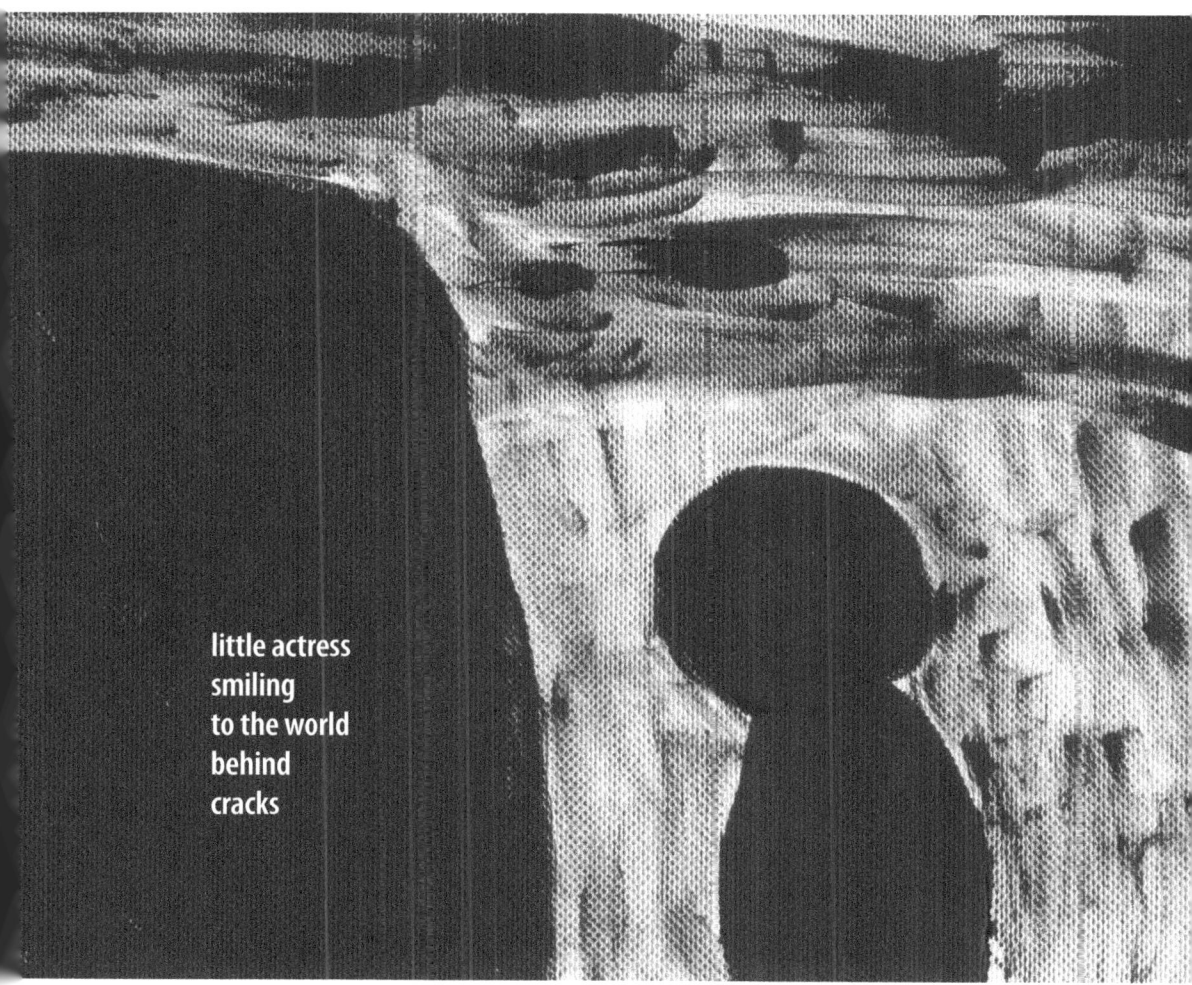

i need to find
distance
from you
currently
leaves a burning
sensation

absence
makes
no sense
as you've
been
there
my entire
life

**don't stare in
the rear view
mirror too long
crash**

i've got to adapt
to the fact
that i'm isolated
alone at home
my phone
becoming
the only window
to the outside
troubled world

holding back the weir
tears ready to burst
and breathe

self conscious
hyper vigilant
exposed

overwhelmed
legs wobbly
sat on floor

acknowledge
they'll never change
grief

let go
surrender
feel

put the whip down
give yourself
a break

mindfulness bell
pause
regulate

take foot
off accelerator
break

if you take
ah
out of empathy
you're left
empty

**shattered
on all levels
surrender**

**anxiety
rises
panic**

**noise
disturbs
peace**

**time
to
exit**

sometimes
you've got
to leave
things behind
lost to you
but found by
someone else
less fortunate
than you are

there is a stone
blocking the doorway
you can choose
to lift it
or remain
stuck
in the past

to witness
the absurdity
in front
of my eyes
try to disguise it
but not able
to eradicate
the scene
unfolding
in front
of me

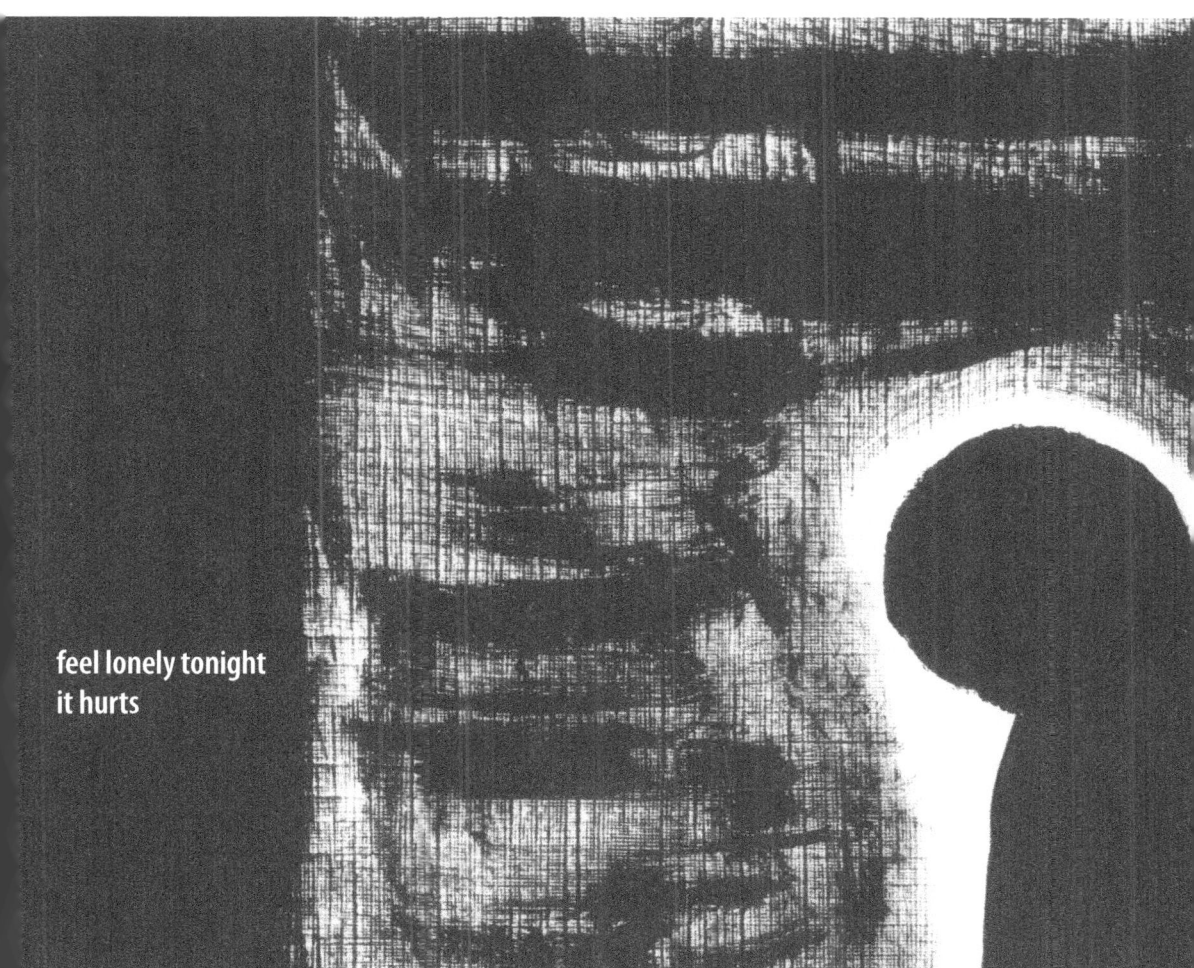

feel lonely tonight
it hurts

a decade has made
me into
who i am
today
it's broken me
challenged me
smashed me
yet i carry on

it's a start
of a new decade
paved
in my own
ways
realising
my dreams
manifesting
them into
reality

i had adjusted to my blindness now i can see for the first time

life is incredulous
and i don't even
know what
the word means

to put pen
on paper
allowing words
to sing
navigating
the landscape

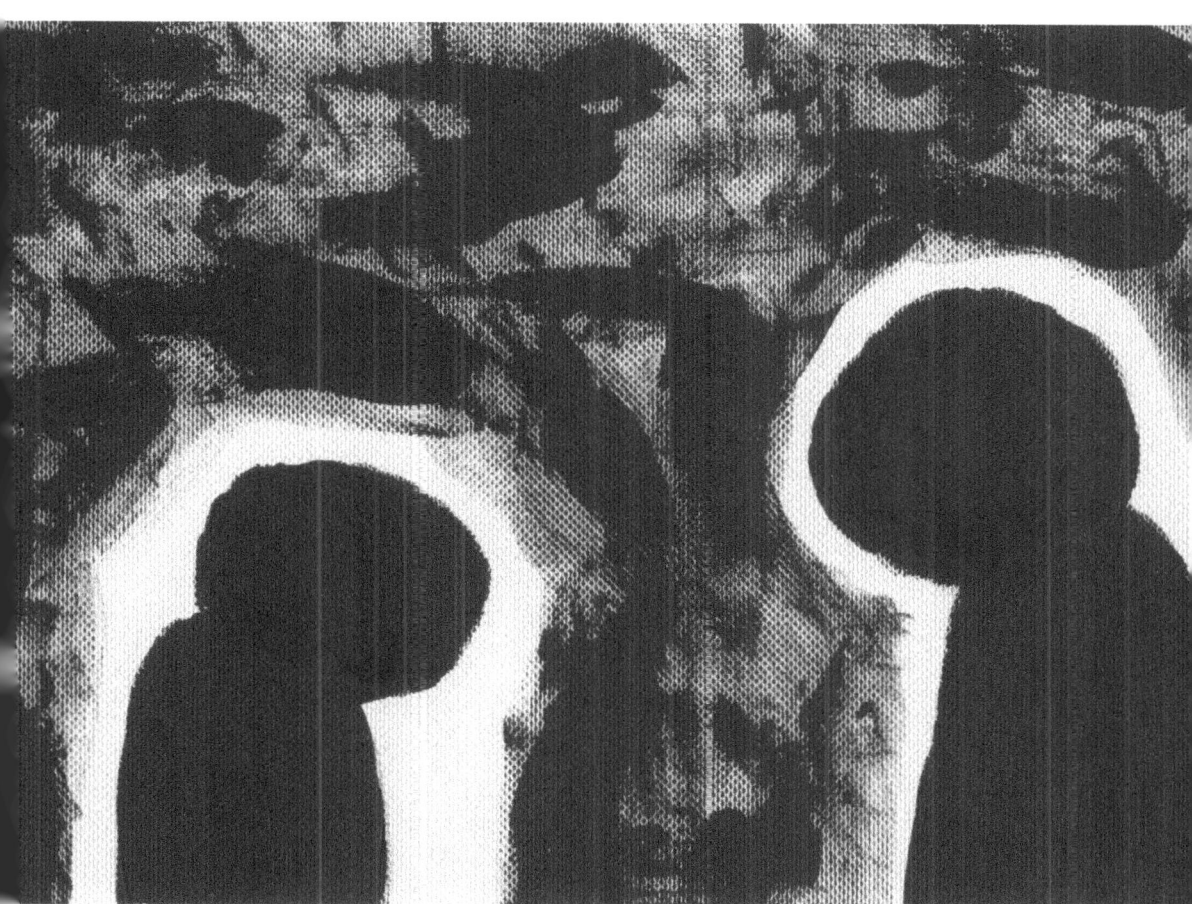

nature
has unearthed
it's self
taken back
control
given birth
to a new
light
language
repairs
momentarily
as we humans
are swept
off our feet

excavate
re-lay
new foundations
to hold
scaffolding
to support
a new structure
trying to be built
from the ashes
of an old building
which doesn't
serve us anymore

just to hear
the birds sing
makes me realise
how lucky i am
to be alive

perhaps
it's not
resentment
i do deserve
respect
and to be
valued
for who
i am

just seeing
your face
gives space
to my feelings
revealing
the sadness
below
the surface

that moment
when you feel
ready
to let go
of someone
or something
you've loved
so dearly
because the pain
of holding on
is insurmountable

isolated
particles
witnessed
by another
remedy
to heal
ripples
outward

overwhelmed
completely
let go

made a mistake
inner critic
screams loudly

standing on my own
two feet
scary

she wants
to control
boundaries

positive
steps forward
sabotage

destructive
nurture
wound

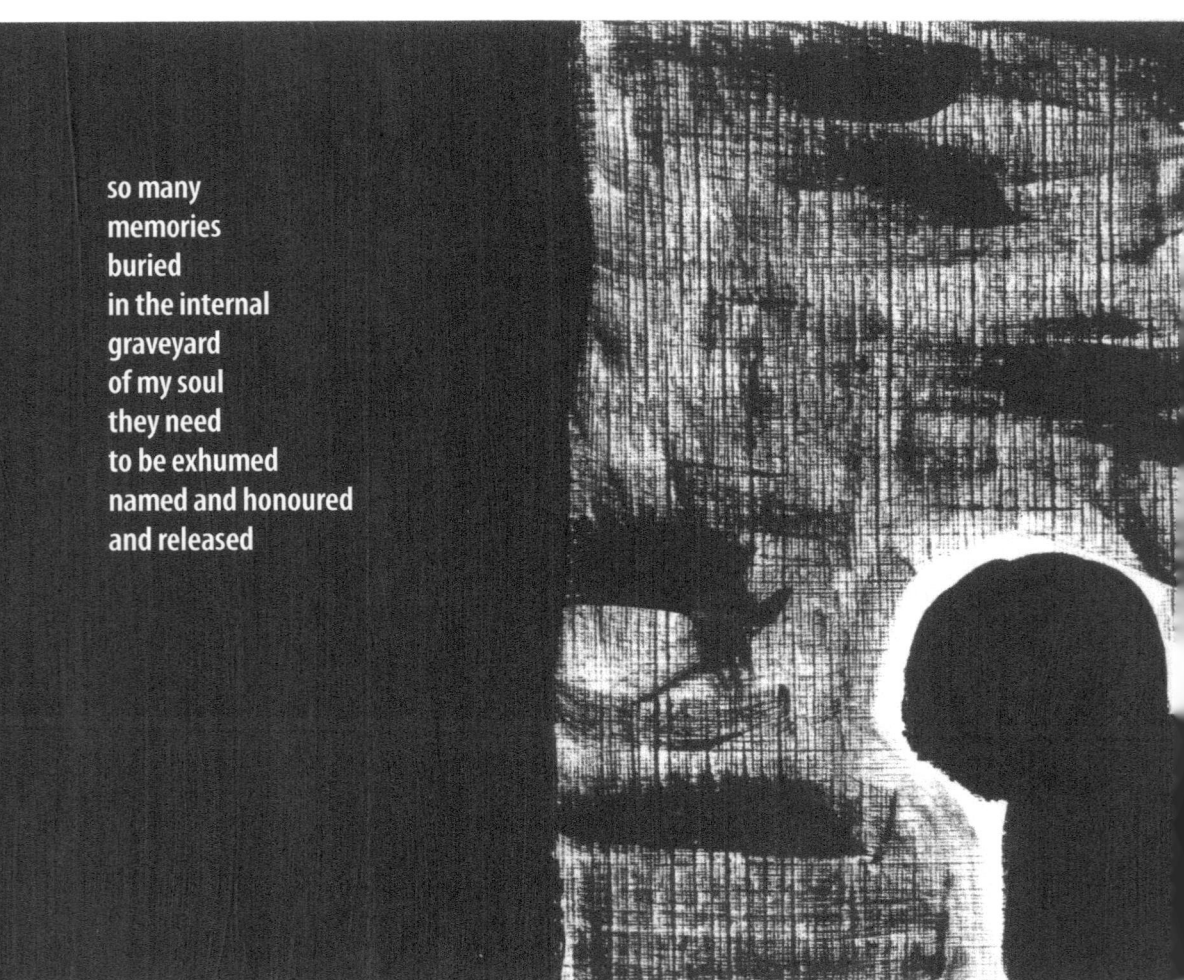

so many
memories
buried
in the internal
graveyard
of my soul
they need
to be exhumed
named and honoured
and released

this room was solitary confinement before

now it's enforced isolation to explore

old memories lingering within these four walls

**nervous system
crashed
flop**

**grief
paralysis
sad**

**loneliness
waves
goodbye**

i needed to switch off
completely give
to me for a change
despite how strange
it may feel
people can survive
without me

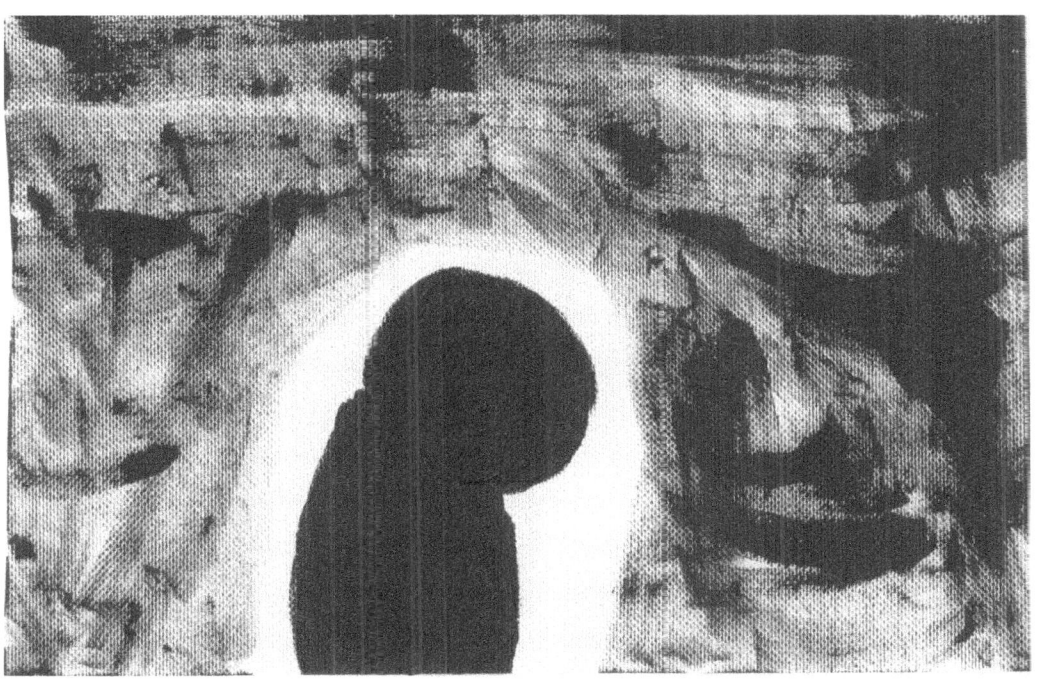

**behind
the smile
was a fractured
self**

masked up
anxious
beneath
the surface
no smile
seen
eyes speak

stepped
out my fortress
escape

change
routine
risk

achieved
so much
awe

self
conscious
alone

how do
you break
the tie
that binds
unites us
yet
leaves
no space
for breath

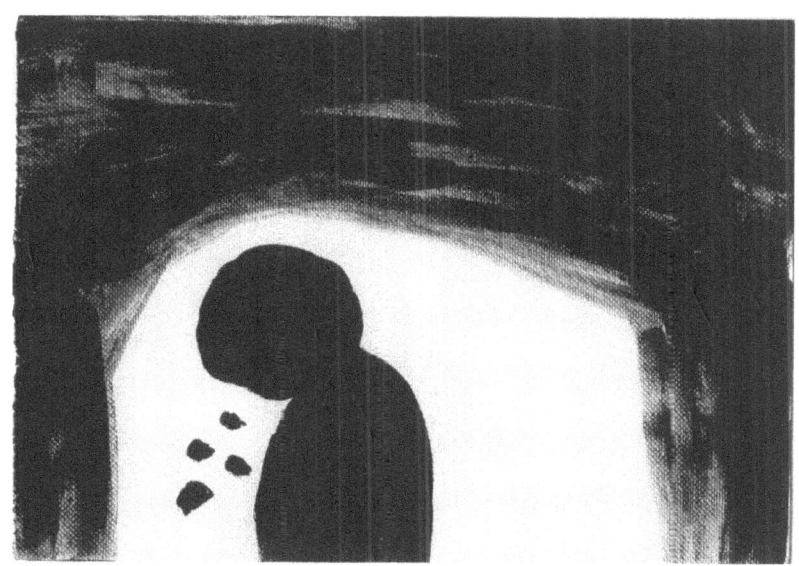

enforced
withdrawal
from society
global crisis
death rises
world aches
cries
wake up

**virtual hug
across zoom
held**

sometimes
there is no
time to
reflect
acceptance

the red
geraniums
bring me solace
vibrant colour
penetrates
my wounded
soul

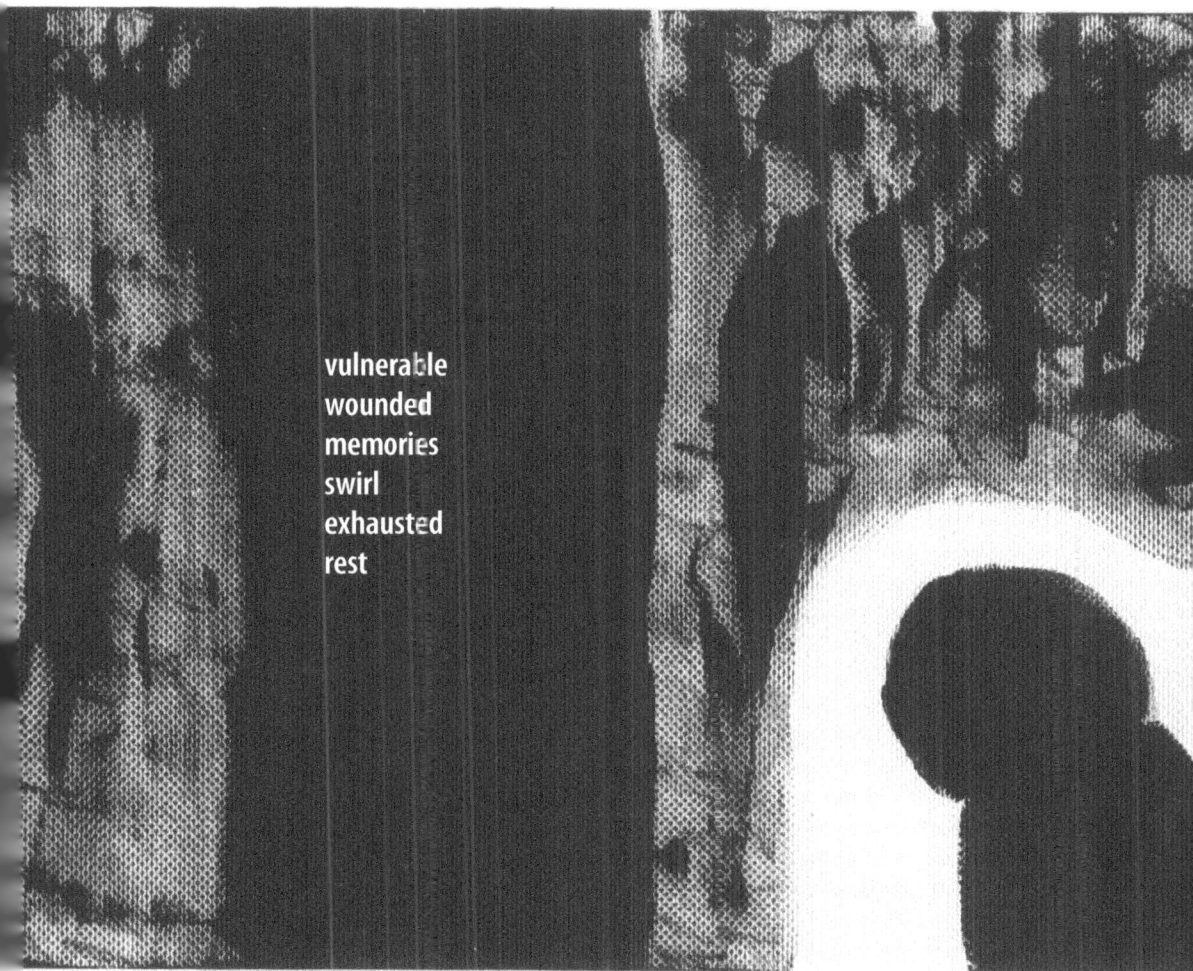

blowing
dandelions
childhood

buttercup
under chin
reflection

**precariously
clinging
onto a ledge
on the edge
of falling
or flying**

and when they
asked her why
she didn't live
her own life
she replied
i didn't deserve it

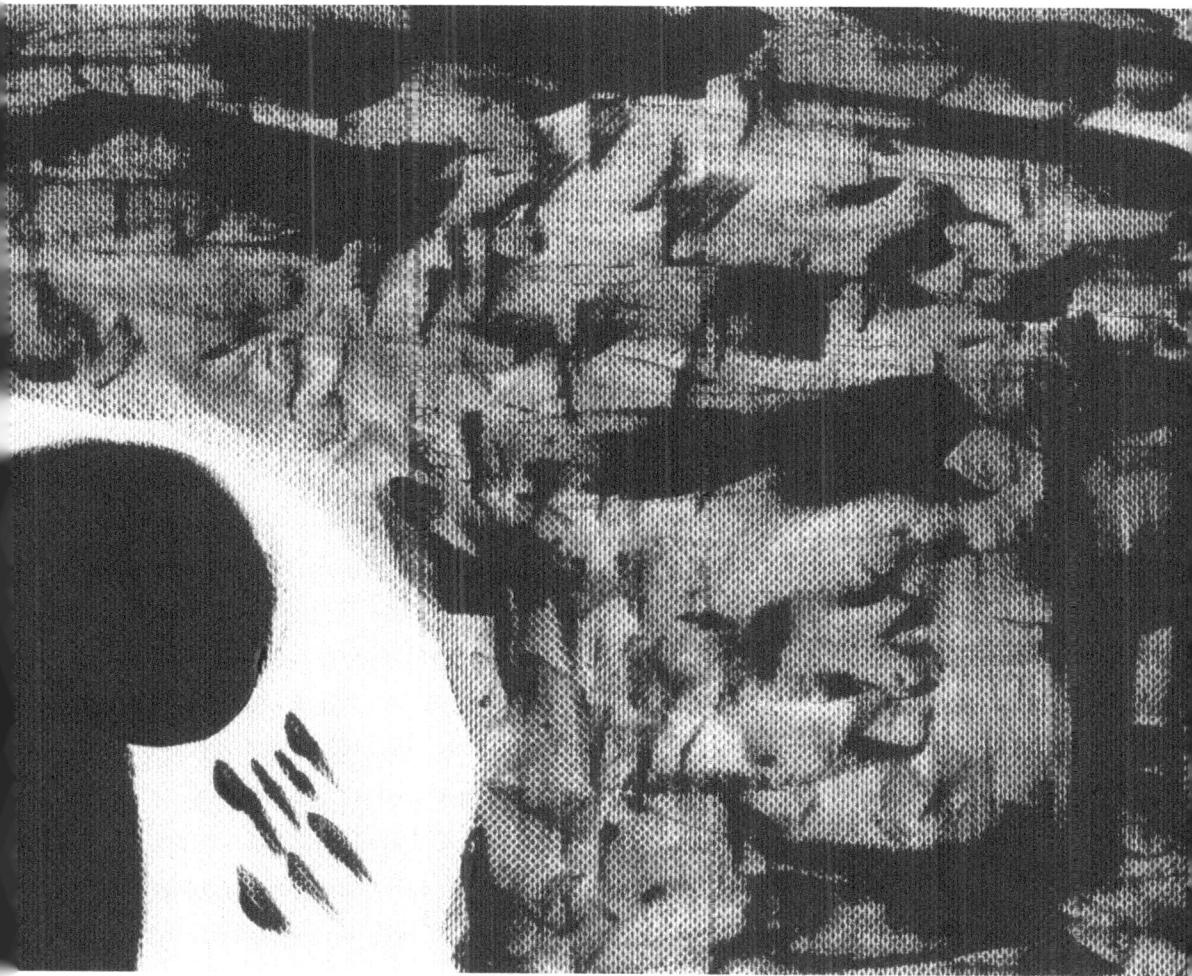

at times the life challenges us to understand something new about ourselves

i don't want
to surround myself
with anyone who
wants to blow
out my light

**do the things you love
because you want to**

turbulence
loss of control
crash

fear
overwhelms
paralysis

trauma
lack of stability
internal war

travelling well
all of a sudden
lost

years of neglect
no choice
wake up

repair damage
child within
scared

sharing thoughts
comforting
release

will it work out
who knows
faith

need to learn
to turn within
for the antidote
to loneliness
it's not possible
to fill that hole
by another

i've hidden
myself
for years
afraid
to allow
anyone in

grieve

super sensitive
triggered
overwhelm

alone
hurt
sad

end of line
sent
virtual hug

stopped
even more tired
necessity
rest

gratitude
strangers
unconditional

limits
reached
pause

a blank page
is made
to be paved
with words
leading
to a path

will there ever
be a time
when i can't
make that
connection
with pen
be able
to anchor
my thoughts
on paper

if i don't
reach out
does anyone
care

watching
her cycle
past my
window
carefree
yet again
stuck
between
grown-up
war
waiting

it's the kindness
of strangers
that restores
my faith
in humanity
people
unknowing
of the joy
they bring
back in my life

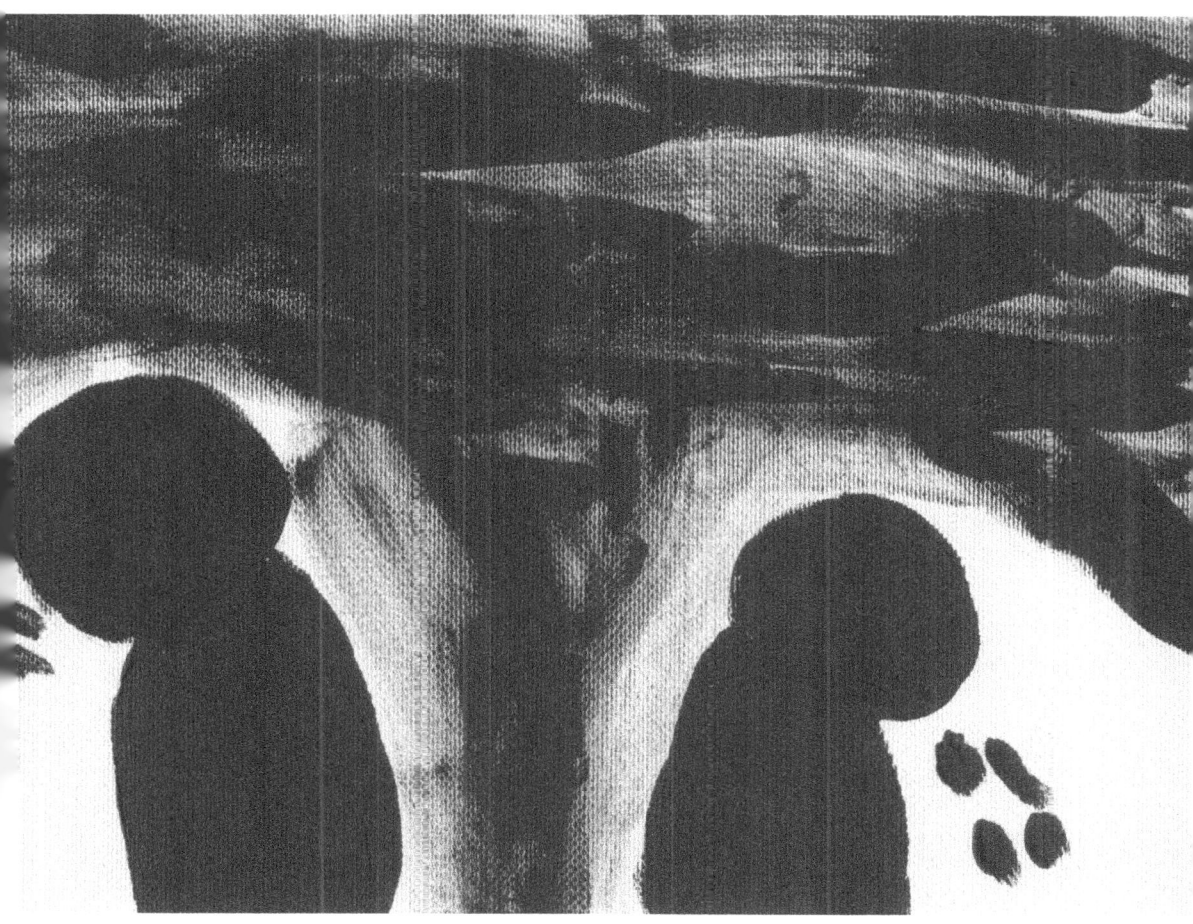

THE SHAPE OF THINGS

As a child I'd stand in the bedroom looking at the different parts of myself spread all over the bed, not knowing how to reassemble myself. There were no instructions. They'd been thrown out long ago. The family I'd come to were isosceles and that was going to prove difficult to me and my geometrical family. They expected me to do what all good isosceles would do. That is get married to an isosceles and have lots of isosceles children, making sure that the first born was a boy triangle. It was necessary for the tribe to carry on. It was important that the race of isosceles did not die out. But the split had been made in the womb. Something happened to me that made me not want to lose that extra angle. I was going to be a square child from the start. This had disturbed my mother and father deeply as they had no arms in which to hold me; that deepened their sadness.

As a child growing up I found it hard to fit in with them. I was a square. Inside myself I felt like a square. I couldn't get involved with their games. It was the way it was. It was a square's nightmare. I was meant to stick with my own kind and not mix with squares, circles, rectangles and hexagons. I found it hard to hold onto my square self. It was so easily contaminated. It wasn't strong enough to say, I'm not like the rest of you. I went under many transformations to try and separate myself and get away from their rules. I began to distort myself. I tried not to see what was going on in front of my eyes: Their disgust for me, their disappointment.

As an adult, separation was not going to be easy. I tried to squeeze myself into their mould, but I couldn't fit my square shoulders into the pattern of their non-existent shoulders. My mother walked in my darkness. She was unconscious of our difference and she tried to shape me into herself. I eclipsed her lines, angles and ideals. My identity did not want to merge with the nuclear family. It was so difficult not to get drawn into their group. I struggled to break out of the pattern. The form and shape of things had to change. She tried everything to make me become isosceles. The more I failed to conform, the more objects were brought into the house to influence me to fit in. On their isosceles TV they'd only watch the Isosceles Channel. The only food and clothes they brought were for triangles. But the food got caught in my throat and the clothes didn't fit my make-up. Finally, they ordered an isosceles door frame. It meant if I didn't get out now, I'd never be able to leave.

walk away sane

www.ingramcontent.com/pod-product-compliance
Lightning Source LLC
Chambersburg PA
CBHW061128070526
44584CB00033B/4256